More One-Hour

MYSTERIES

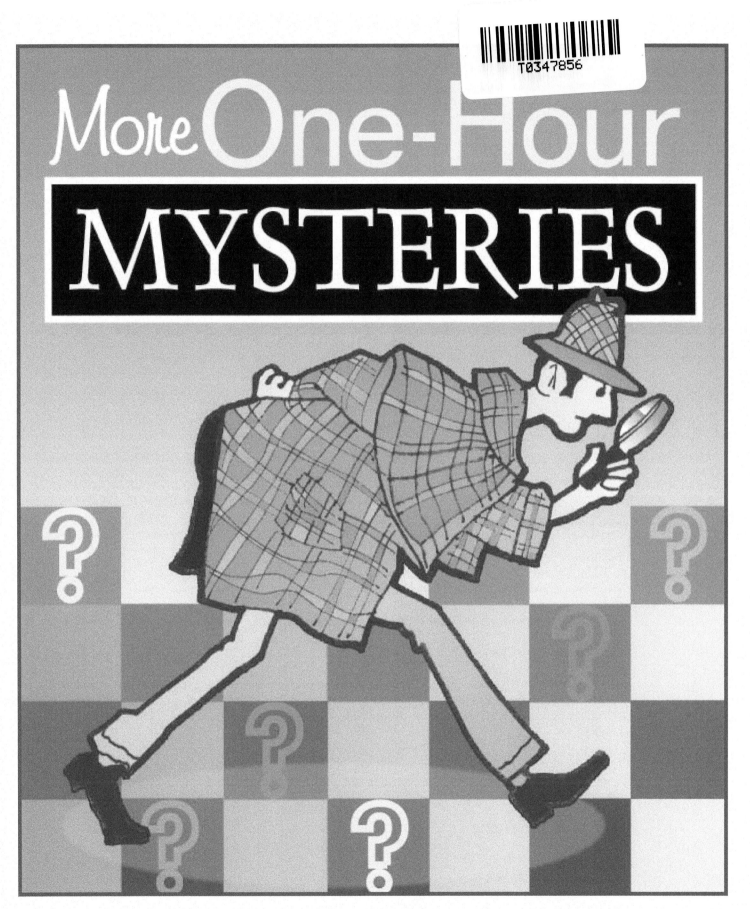

Written by **Mary Ann Carr**   ❖   Illustrated by **Stephanie O'Shaughnessy**

Dedicated to my nine
great nieces and nephews

First published in 2005 by Prufrock Press Inc.

Published in 2021 by Routledge
605 Third Avenue, New York, NY 10017
2 Park Square, Milton Park, Abingdon, Oxon OX14 4RN

Routledge is an imprint of the Taylor & Francis Group, an informa business

ISBN: 9781593631093 (pbk)

DOI: 10.4324/9781003236740

Contents

Introduction

In *More One Hour Mysteries*, students will once again think like detectives when they uncover the culprits in robberies, a dognapping, a forgery, and a hoax. They will investigate suspects, determine their motives, and substantiate their alibis. In addition, they will examine a variety of other clues critical to each case, all of which lead to the guilty party.

There are five mysteries in this book, each one requiring students to use deductive reasoning skills, draw inferences, take notes, and organize data as they analyze the evidence and eliminate the suspects one by one from the suspect list. Each mystery includes complete instructions for the teacher and attractive reproducible pages for students, providing the clues and data they need to solve each crime.

Miss Moneybags's Last Will and Testament

This mystery takes student detectives to the Moneybags mansion where they will uncover the culprit who stole the dying woman's last will. They will discover clues by solving a variety of logic puzzles, each providing a key to the mystery's solution.

The Doggone Mystery

Dog lovers will enjoy investigating the disappearance of Bugle Bones, the Safety Spaniel, star of T.V. Student detectives will examine physical evidence left at the crime scene to determine which of the six suspects dognapped this famous canine.

The Case of the Forged Houdini

If you need a thought-provoking Halloween project, this is it. The case takes place at a costume party on Halloween night. After analyzing the signature of the great magician and determining that a forgery has occurred, student detectives will solve the crime by uncovering clues, all of which point to the one guilty guest.

Who Took the Video Game?

Hold on to your joy sticks and get ready to solve a mystery that begins when a computer expert discovers that his design for a sensational new product, a holographic video game, has been stolen. Student detectives will investigate other computer experts who are the suspects and will gather evidence found at the crime scene – footprints and two coded messages.

Aunt Sally's Secret

Whether you have a mysterious relative or not, you'll enjoy solving this case. The mystery takes students to a middle school where a culprit has staged a hoax. Student detectives will analyze documents in order to validate the hoax as well as investigate a list of suspects to determine "who done it."

Teachers may choose to use this book in a variety of ways. The crimes may be included in a single unit on mysteries or logical thinking. Teachers might also want their students to solve one crime every six weeks. Each mystery requires approximately one hour to solve. The longer mysteries, however, could be extended into two class periods.

In addition to the clever mysteries, supplementary activities are included for some of the stories. These activities can add information about investigative procedures.

Happy Sleuthing!

Miss Moneybags's Last Will and Testament
Teacher's Guide

The Introduction

Hand out the first page of the mystery (page 8) and ask students to read the newspaper article and the section marked "The Crime." Discuss the crime and the questions listed at the bottom of the page. Discuss reasons the will might have been stolen.

Answers

The beneficiaries in the first will are likely suspects. A beneficiary might be afraid Miss Moneybags eliminated them from the last will or worried that the amount to be received in the last will is less than in the first will. The will was stolen between 1:45 p.m. and 4:00 p.m., when Mr. Beam arrived.

The Suspects

Tell students that in solving this mystery, they will think like detectives as they analyze clues and make deductions in order to solve a variety of logic puzzles. The solution to each puzzle provides pertinent information about the case.

Hand out "The Beneficiaries" sheet (page 9). Ask students to complete the matrix logic puzzle in order to determine how much Miss Moneybags's nephew, friend and employees were to receive in her first will.

Answer

nephew - $15 million	*cook - $75,000*
secretary - $500,000	*housekeeper - $100,000*
director - $10 million	*chauffeur - $20 million*
butler - $5 million	*best friend - jewelry*

After completing the puzzle, discuss who had a motive and why. Miss Moneybags's best friend has no motive to steal the will because she is as wealthy as Miss Moneybags. All other beneficiaries have a motive as discussed in the introduction.

Hand out "The Suspects" (page 10). Read the statements made by the nurse and Mr. Beam regarding hostility between Miss Moneybags and the suspects. Discuss the questions. The statements reveal that many of the beneficiaries had a recent conflict with Miss Moneybags. As a result, they might fear a change in her will.

Answer

Based on the evidence that the chauffeur was devoted to Miss Moneybags, never quarreled with her and had no reason to think she would eliminate him from her new will, he has no motive to steal the second will. He can be eliminated as a suspect.

The Alibi

Explain to students that now that they have suspects with a motive, they need to determine if any of them were in the mansion between 1:45 p.m. and 4:00 p.m.

Hand out "Who Had the Opportunity?" (page 11). Ask students to complete the matrix logic puzzle to discover the last name of each suspect and when he or she arrived at the mansion. Remind students that all of them were in the mansion the day Miss Moneybags died.

Answer

> *nephew - Tull - 11:30 a.m.* *butler - Byrd - 10:00 a.m.*
> *secretary - Free - 4:20 p.m.* *housekeeper - Hill - 8:00 a.m.*
> *director - Whit - 12:25 p.m.* *cook - Grey - 8:30 a.m.*
>
> *Based on this evidence, the secretary can be eliminated. She arrived at the mansion after the will was discovered missing.*

More Evidence

Explain that with the motive and alibi established, Detective Basse must find more evidence to discover the guilty culprit. Hand out "An Afternoon Treat" (page 12). Explain that this is a different type of logic puzzle. It is called a table logic puzzle, requiring the students to determine where each of the suspects were sitting at the table while having an afternoon treat. They also must determine what type of snack each suspect was eating. Ask them to read the sheet to determine why this information is important to the case. Discuss. Then, ask students to complete the puzzle.

Answer

>   director
>   *Incredible Squares*
>
> cook   housekeeper
> *Mysterious Treats*   *Coconut Delights*
>
>   nephew   butler
>   *Tasty Dandies*   *Chocolate Bites*

Hand out "Bite Delight Recipes" (page 13). Ask students to examine the recipes to determine who might have left traces of powdered sugar in the drawer.

Answer

> *The director, housekeeper, cook, and nephew were eating treats dipped in powdered sugar and therefore could have left traces of it in the drawer. The butler can be eliminated*

After Snack Activities

Tell students that this clue not only narrows down the suspect list, it also narrows down the time the will was taken. The time of the crime had to be after 2:30 p.m. The suspects went to the dining room for a snack at 2:00 p.m. and stayed for 30 minutes.

Hand out "Caught in a Lie" (page 14). Tell students that by solving this puzzle they will catch one of the suspects in a lie. Instruct students to first review the time during the day that the suspects arrived at the mansion. Using this data and the results from the logic puzzle, they can determine who was lying. Ask students to solve the logic puzzle.

Answer

director	*sun room*	*reading*	*butler*
nephew	*den*	*watching T.V.*	*secretary*
housekeeper	*living room*	*puzzle*	*friend*
cook	*dining room*	*journal writing*	*chauffeur*

Tell students that Detective Basse thought he knew who had stolen the will based on the evidence he had accumulated. Ask students who they think might have done it. What evidence do they have to substantiate their idea? Discuss their ideas.

Who was lying?
> *the nephew*

How do they know?
> *He claimed that the secretary had been with him in the den; however, she didn't arrive at the mansion until 4:20 p.m.*

Epilogue

Tell students that Detective Basse called everyone into the library. "I know who is guilty," he said. When he pointed to the nephew, the man stood up and started to run from the room. Detective Basse grabbed him and forced him to put both hands on the wall. He motioned for Mr. Beam to search his pockets. He found the will, still sealed in an envelope, in his suit coat pocket.

Mr. Beam opened the envelope and pulled out the will. After reading it, he began to laugh. Then, he read what was written on the paper.

Miss Moneybag's Last Will and Testament

This will is unusual in that my only request is this. If at the time of my death, this will can still be found in the desk drawer where the nurse placed it, all things written in my first will remain as I requested. If, on the other hand, this will is missing, then I request that those responsible for its loss be taken out of my first will and, therefore, receive nothing. His or her portion of the will shall be divided equally among all of the other beneficiaries.

> *Signed,*
> *Marybeth Moneybags*

The Moral

Crime doesn't pay and neither does greed. Be thankful for what you have and spend your money wisely.

Miss Moneybags's Last Will and Testament

A Newspaper Article

Obituaries
Marybeth Moneybags

Miss Marybeth Moneybags, heir to the Moneybags family fortune, died of natural causes in her home Thursday afternoon. She was ninety-nine years old. Her father, Cornelius Moneybags, was the founder of Bite Delight Cookie Company. His famous cookie, the Merry Chocolate Bite, established him as a leader in the baking industry.

Miss Moneybags resided at the Moneybags Mansion, the family estate near Boston, Massachusetts. A noted philanthropist, Miss Moneybags established the Moneybags Foundation in 1970. Since that time, the Foundation has given millions of dollars to many charitable organizations.

The Crime

When Miss Moneybags died, her nurse raced downstairs to call Miss Moneybags's attorney, Rufus Beam.

"She wanted you to know that she had written a new will. She wrote it this afternoon," the nurse told Mr. Beam when he arrived at the mansion fifteen minutes later. "After she wrote it, she sealed it in an envelope and asked me to take it downstairs and put it in this desk drawer. It was 1:45 p.m. when I put the will in the drawer. Then I returned to Miss Moneybags's room. She was asleep. She died at 3:45 p.m."

When Rufus Beam asked the nurse to get the will from the desk drawer, she was horrified to find that it wasn't there. "Someone has taken it!" she exclaimed.

⇨ **Who might have stolen the will?**_____

⇨ **Why might someone want to steal it?**_____

⇨ **When was it stolen?**_____

The Beneficiaries

Mr. Beam called his friend Detective Hayden Basse at police headquarters and asked him to meet him at the Moneybags estate. Upon his arrival, Detective Basse learned that in her first will, Miss Moneybags had made bequests to her nephew, her best friend, and some of her employees. All other property and money would go to the Moneybags Foundation. Her last will made the day of her death, however, would be the will that would be honored.

When Detective Basse read the first will, he discovered that Miss Moneybags had been more generous with some of the people than with others. Solve the logic puzzle to determine how much she planned to leave each person in the first will.

	jewelry	$75,000	$100,000	$500,000	$5 million	$10 million	$15 million	$20 million
nephew								
secretary								
director								
butler								
cook								
housekeeper								
chauffeur								
friend								

Clues

1. The chauffeur was to receive the most money.
2. Miss Moneybags planned to leave the butler millions of dollars.
3. The housekeeper would get less than the secretary.
4. Her best friend, who was as wealthy as Miss Moneybags, was to receive only her jewelry.
5. The cook would get either seventy-five thousand or ten million dollars.
6. The housekeeper was disappointed she wouldn't get millions.
7. The director would get more than the butler but less than the nephew.

 Who had a motive to steal the will? _____

 Was there anyone who didn't? _____

The Suspects

Detective Basse asked the nurse and Rufus Beam if any of the beneficiaries knew about the new will. He also asked if either of them had detected any hostility between Miss Moneybags and the beneficiaries. Detective Basse recorded their statements.

✏️ Detective Basse's Notes

Nurse	The housekeeper was in the library when I put the will in the desk drawer. I told her Miss Moneybags had just written it. That housekeeper is such a gossip, I'm sure she told everyone about it. Actually, Miss Moneybags was always fussing at her about gossiping.
	I overheard an argument several days ago between Miss Moneybags and her nephew. She told him that he was spending money recklessly. "It doesn't grow on trees," she said.
	I never heard the chauffeur quarrel with anyone. He's very kind. In fact, even though Miss Moneybags hasn't needed him since she became ill three months ago, he has come here every day to check on her.
Mr. Beam	I informed everyone who was at the house that sadly Miss Moneybags had passed on. Everyone seemed to already know that there was a new will.
	Yesterday when I came to the mansion, I found the secretary crying her eyes out in the parlor. When I asked what was wrong, she said that she could never please anyone, especially Miss Moneybags.
	The butler told me he was worried Miss Moneybags wasn't happy with him because he had recently taken a long vacation.
	The cook and Miss Moneybags have always been at odds.
	The director and Miss Moneybags had a disagreement about an issue at the Foundation. Just last week Miss Moneybags said she was not happy at all with a decision he had made.

👉 **Why is it important to know if any of the beneficiaries knew about the will?**

_____

👉 **Why did Detective Basse want to know if any of the beneficiaries had a conflict with Miss Moneybags?** _____

👉 **Who does not seem to have a motive to steal the will?** _____

Who Had the Opportunity?

Detective Basse asked each of the six remaining suspects what time during the day they arrived at the Moneybags mansion. Complete the logic puzzle to determine the name of each suspect and the time they arrived at the mansion.

	Byrd	Grey	Hill	Whit	Free	Tull	8:00 a.m.	8:30 a.m.	10:00 a.m.	11:30 a.m.	12:25 p.m.	4:20 p.m.
nephew												
secretary												
director												
butler												
housekeeper												
cook												
8:00 a.m.												
8:30 a.m.												
10:00 a.m.												
11:30 a.m.												
12:25 p.m.												
4:20 p.m.												

Clues

1. Byrd arrived at 10:00 a.m. after Hill and Grey.

2. Whit arrived at 12:25 p.m. before the secretary.

3. The housekeeper, whose name is neither Grey or Free, arrived first.

4. The butler arrived after the cook but before the nephew, whose name is Tull.

☞ **How does this information help Detective Basse?** _____

_____

☞ **Based on this evidence, can he eliminate anyone as a suspect?** _____

_____

An Afternoon Treat

After questioning the suspects, Detective Basse examined the drawer in and around the bedside table, searching for even the tiniest clue that might have been left behind. He found traces of a white powder inside the drawer, which the forensics lab analyzed and concluded was powdered sugar. He asked the butler if anyone had eaten a snack in the house that afternoon.

The butler informed him that he, the housekeeper, the butler, the cook, and the nephew had met in the dining room at 2:00 p.m. for an afternoon snack. "We were all here for about 30 minutes." The detective then asked everyone to come to the dining room and sit where they had sat earlier. He also asked them to get the same treat that they had eaten for their snack.

Solve the logic puzzle to determine where each of these suspects (the butler, the director, the nephew, the housekeeper, and the cook) sat and what type of snack they ate.

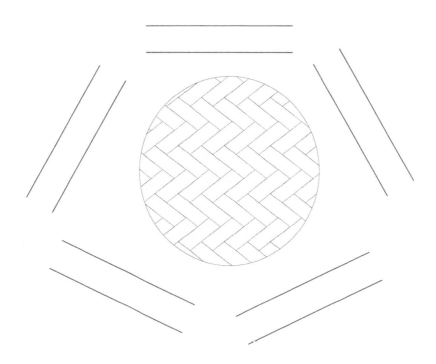

Clues

1. The director, who ate Incredible Squares, sat to the left of the cook.
2. The housekeeper sat to the right of the person who ate Chocolate Bites.
3. The person who ate Tasty Dandies sat between the butler and the cook.
4. The housekeeper ate Coconut Delights.
5. The person who ate Mysterious Treat sat next to the person who ate Incredible Squares.

Bite Delight Recipes

Read the recipes for these Bite Delight treats to determine which suspect might have left traces of powdered sugar beside the desk.

Mysterious Treat

1 c. shortening	2 eggs
1 c. brown sugar	1 tsp. vanilla
1 c. white sugar	1 c. crushed potato chips
1 T. baking soda	¾ c. nuts

Cream shortening, sugar and eggs until creamy. Add remaining ingredients. Mix. Drop by teaspoons onto cookie sheet and slightly flatten with a fork. Bake at 350° for 10 minutes. Cool. Dust with powdered sugar.

Chocolate Bites

1 c. butter	2 tsp. vanilla
¾ c. sugar	2 ½ c. flour
¾ c. brown sugar	½ tsp. salt
2 eggs	1 tsp. baking soda
2 c. flour	24 oz. chocolate chips

Cream butter and sugar. Add eggs and vanilla. Beat in flour, salt, and soda. Fold in chocolate chips. Bake at 375° on an ungreased sheet for 8-10 minutes.

ଓ ଓ ଓ ଓ ଓ

Tasty Dandies

1 c. butter	1 T. vanilla
4 T. powdered sugar	powdered sugar
2 c. flour	1 ½ tsp. baking powder

Cream butter and sugar. Add flour, baking powder and salt. Add vanilla and nuts. Drop in one inch balls on a greased cookie sheet. Bake at 375° until brown. Roll in powdered sugar.

Coconut Delights

2 sticks butter	1 tsp. vanilla
1 ½ c. sugar	1-3 oz. coconut
2 c. flour	powdered sugar

Cream butter and sugar. Add flour, vanilla and coconut. Roll into small balls. Put on a cookie sheet. Flatten with a fork. Bake at 350° for 20-25 minutes. Cool and dust with powdered sugar.

✳ ✳ ✳ ✳ ✳

Incredible Squares

½ stick butter	¾ c. chopped nuts
1 c. sugar	¾ c. chocolate syrup
3 eggs	powdered sugar
2 c. flour	dash of salt

Cream butter and sugar. Add eggs. Add flour and salt to the creamed mixture. Add chopped nuts, chocolate syrup and vanilla. Pour into greased and floured 9-inch square pan. Bake at 350° for 35 minutes. Cool. Sprinkle with powdered sugar.

Which suspects might have left traces of the powder?

Caught In a Lie

Detective Basse asked the four prime suspects where they were between 2:30 and 4:00 p.m. The suspects said that after their snack they became engaged in an activity in one of the rooms in the mansion. They all claimed someone had been with them and could substantiate their alibi.

Solve the logic puzzle to determine where the suspects spent time, the activity they were engaged in, and the people who could substantiate their alibis.

	location				activity				substantiated by			
	den	living	dining	sun room	puzzle	reading	journal	T.V.	chauffeur	butler	secretary	friend
director												
nephew												
housekeeper												
cook												
chauffeur												
butler												
secretary												
friend												

Clues

1. The cook said she remained in the dining room to write in her journal.
2. The suspect in the den said he watched T.V. with the secretary.
3. The housekeeper loved to work puzzles.
4. The director was in the sunroom with the butler but was not watching T.V.
5. The friend was knitting in the living room next to the person doing puzzles.
6. The chauffeur said he was not with the person watching T.V.

After Detective Basse talked with the suspects, he knew that one of them was lying and, therefore, most likely was the person who stole the will.

 Who was lying? How did the detective know it was a lie? _____

THE DOGGONE MYSTERY
Teacher's Guide

Introduction

Hand out the introduction (page 17) for students to read. Discuss the crime. Refer students to the detective notes and ask them to fill in the information that is available to them in the introduction. Discuss why it is important for detectives to take detailed notes when working on a case.

The Suspects

Hand out the "Suspect List" (page 18). Ask the students to read this page. Discuss the motive that each of the suspects might have.

Answer
- *The suspects might be jealous because Bugle Bones was a star or because Mr. Filibuster won the award.*
- *Revenge because Bugle Bones kept their dog from getting the role.*
- *Revenge because Mr. Filibuster won the Golden Paw award instead of another trainer.*

Which suspect has no motive?

Answer
- *Maggie Basse has no motive. She has no reason to be unhappy because Bugle Bones won the part or because Mr. Filibuster won the award.*
- *She has no reason to do either of them harm and there is no indication that she needs the money.*

The Alibi

Read the alibis (page 19). Discuss the fact that for an alibi to be substantiated it needs to be backed up or verified.

Ask students to jot down their ideas in the "Detective Notes" on the bottom of the page. Discuss.

Answer
- *Maggie Basse and Nicole Williamson have alibis that could be substantiated.*
- *Harvey Hepple's physics teacher could substantiate that there was a physics test. If Harvey was alone that evening, however, there would be no one to confirm the fact that he studied for it.*
- *Loose Draw could verify that he rented videos and bought doughnuts; however, if he lives alone, there might not be anyone to confirm that he stayed home and watched the movies.*
- *Ruffin's and Listwell's alibis could only be confirmed if they had spent the entire evening with someone who could prove that they had not gone to the kennel.*

Confirming the Alibis

Read and discuss "Confirming the Alibis" (page 20). Complete the "Detective Notes" on the bottom of the page.

Answer
Both Maggie Basse and Nicole Williamson have alibis that were substantiated, so both should be eliminated from the suspect list.

A Paper Clue

Hand out " A Paper Clue" (page 21). Ask students to read and complete the puzzle and the detective notes.

Answer

Harvey Hepple - Wally World - laptop
Roscoe Ruffin - Office Works - desktop
Felix Listwell - Paper King - electric typewriter
Loose Draw - Buy A Lot - portable typewriter

Discuss detective notes.

Answer

The fact that the suspect owned paper that was the same type as that on which the note was written indicates that the suspect could have written the note. It is unlikely that Loose Draw wrote the note. He should, therefore, be eliminated from the list unless further evidence points to him.

Fingerprints

Hand out "Fingerprints" (page 22). Ask students to analyze the prints and then answer the question at the bottom of the page. Discuss.

Answer

- *Although Harvey had reason to be at the kennel, therefore, making it logical that his prints would be found there, we cannot eliminate him as a suspect. He still could have committed the crime. He had a motive and no alibi.*
- *Roscoe Ruffin's prints were not found at the kennel. This does not necessarily mean, however, that he did not commit the crime. He could have worn gloves or wiped his fingerprints off of all the surfaces that he touched. He also had a motive and no alibi.*
- *Felix Listwell's prints were found at the scene. This is circumstantial evidence. This type of evidence implies that a suspect might be guilty. It does not, however, prove it. The fact that Listwell's prints were found at the kennel places him there at some point in time. But it does not prove he was there the night of the crime. Because he could not establish a reason for ever being at the kennel, however, his prints imply that he might be the culprit.*

See the supplementary activities in the back of the book for more activities involving fingerprints.

A Tool Impression

Hand out "A Tool Impression" (page 23). Tell students that every tool is unique. Each one has different striations (lines) caused during the manufacturing process and defects as a result of wear and tear. Ask students to analyze the photographs of the tools owned by the three suspects and compare them to the "jimmy" mark found on the door jamb.

Ask students who they think committed the crime and what evidence they have to support their idea. List the evidence on the board.

Answer

Felix Listwell is the culprit. He had a motive and no alibi. He owned paper like that on which the ransom note was written. His fingerprints place him at the crime scene and the "jimmy" mark matched the striations on his crowbar.

Epilogue

Listwell was arrested and confessed. He stated that he didn't know what had come over him and that he was sorry for the pain he caused Mr. Filibuster. Bugle Bones and Mr. Filibuster were overjoyed to be reunited.

THE DOGGONE MYSTERY

1st Place

Arnold Filibuster is famous for training dogs for television commercials. His most famous dog is Bugle Bones, the celebrity dog used for Hearty Meal Dog Food commercials. As a result of his popularity across the nation, Bugle Bones was recently cast as the star of the new T.V. adventure series, *Bugle Bones, the Safety Spaniel.*

Last evening, Mr. Filibuster went to the annual awards dinner for dog trainers where he received the coveted Golden Paw, an award for dog trainer of the year. He visited his kennel just before he left for the dinner at 6:00 p.m. All the dogs, including Bugle Bones, were safely in their cages. When he returned home at 9:30 p.m., he went to the kennel to check on the dogs. He was alarmed to find the gate of the chain link fence that surrounded the kennel wide open. Then he saw that the door to the kennel was open too. He remembered locking it before he left for dinner.

He spotted a typewritten note taped to the door frame. It read, "If you ever want to see your precious star alive, do **NOT** call police. Just give me my price. I'll contact you later." Mr. Filibuster raced to his favorite spaniel's cage. The door was open. Bugle Bones was missing!

Despite the warning, Mr. Filibuster called police. Detective Barkmore, the detective assigned to the case, raced over. Like all good detectives, he kept detailed notes about his cases, so he started immediately recording all the facts.

☞ **Help Detective Barkmore find the guilty culprit. Record facts of the case you have at this point.**

Detective Notes

What was the crime? _____

Where did it happen? _____

When did it happen? _____

How did the culprit get into the kennel? <u>More investigation is needed to</u>

<u>determine how the culprit got into the kennel when the door was locked.</u>

<u>The gate had no lock.</u>

SUSPECT LIST

After questioning people who knew about Bugle Bones and his recent success, Detective Barkmore compiled a list of suspects.

Harvey Hepple
Hepple has worked for Mr. Filibuster for three years as a kennel attendant. It is his responsibility to care for the dogs, feeding and walking them each day. In addition, he cleans the kennels. He is a college student and had recently asked Mr. Filibuster for a raise. When Filibuster said he couldn't give him a raise, he threatened to quit, but then changed his mind.

Maggie Basse
Basse is a dog lover who worked for Mr. Filibuster for three years until she recently got married. She was thrilled that Bugle Bones got the part.

Roscoe Ruffin
Ruffin has trained dogs for years. His dogs are successful in commercials; however, he has never had one who starred in a T.V. show or movie. When he heard about Bugle Bones's success, he was angry. He told Mr. Filibuster that Bugle Bones was no better than any dog he had ever trained.

Nicole Williamson
Williamson owns many dogs used in commercials. She has dreamed for years of having one of her dogs star in a T.V. series. She was hoping that her Brittany spaniel would get the role Bugle Bones got.

Felix Listwell
Listwell is a dog trainer. He has recently had bad luck with his dogs. One of them bit a director while making a commercial and the company fired the dog. Listwell took his favorite dog, a blond cocker spaniel, to the Safety spaniel auditions and was upset when the dog didn't get the part.

Loose Draw
Loose Draw is a known thief, specializing in stealing pedigreed dogs and selling them. He had recently served time for stealing an award-winning poodle. Upon his release from prison, he told the warden that he had reformed and would never steal again.

 Are any of these suspects lacking a motive? If so, who? _____

ALIBIS

Detective Barkmore questioned the suspects to find out where they were on the night of the crime. They gave the following alibis.

Harvey Hepple "I was at home, studying for a big test in physics."

Maggie Basse "My husband and I had a dinner party that evening for two other couples. Our company arrived at six o'clock and didn't leave until twelve-thirty."

Roscoe Ruffin "I was supposed to go to a dinner for dog trainers, but I was home sick with an upset stomach."

Nicole Williamson "I was at a fundraiser for the local S.P.C.A. I'm president of the board, you know."

Felix Listwell "I was home alone and didn't do anything except watch a little T.V. before I went to bed early, around nine o'clock."

Loose Draw "I rented some videos from Star Video around six, stopped at Dunk A Doughnut and got a dozen doughnuts, came home and ate doughnuts while I watched the movies."

"It looks like only a couple of these alibis are likely to be backed up or substantiated," Detective Barkmore said.

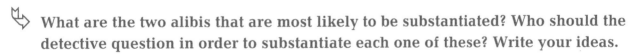 **What are the two alibis that are most likely to be substantiated? Who should the detective question in order to substantiate each one of these? Write your ideas.**

Detective Notes

_____

_____

_____

CONFIRMING THE ALIBIS

Harvey Hepple   Harvey's physics teacher confirmed that there was a big test the day after the crime. Hepple lives alone in an apartment near the college. No one saw him study or contacted him that evening by phone. His apartment is a 45-minute drive from Mr. Filibuster's house.

Maggie Basse   Mr. Basse's boss stated that he and his wife spent the evening with the Basses. "We got there promptly at 6:00," he said, "and left at 12:30."

Roscoe Ruffin   Ruffin lives alone in a house located six blocks from Mr. Filibuster.

Nicole Williamson   The vice-president of the S.P.C.A. board of directors stated that Williamson was at the fundraiser. "She and I both got there around 5:30 to get everything ready for the dinner at 7:00. We both left at 10:30 p.m."

Felix Listwell   Felix lives in a rented house, 12 miles from Mr. Filibuster's kennel. It is a 20-minute drive.

Loose Draw   The clerk at Star Video verified that Loose Draw had rented three videos at six o'clock. Loose Draw had a receipt from Dunk A Doughnut for a dozen powdered sugar doughnuts. The time recorded on the receipt was 6:15 p.m. The doughnut shop is across the street from Star Video. The drive from Star Video to Mr. Fillibuster's house takes 15 minutes.

 Based on their alibis, which suspects aren't guilty?

Detective Notes
_____
_____
_____

A PAPER CLUE

The forensic experts examined the ransom note from Bugle Bones's kennel. After the analysis was complete, Detective Barkmore received the following report:

> The paper on which the note was written is multipurpose paper — 20 pound weight with a 90 brightness. It is sold in Wally World, Office Works and Paper King but not in Buy-A-Lot Discount Stores.

Barkmore investigated each of the remaining suspects' homes. He found that each one had paper matching the analysis. He asked to see the receipts where they bought the paper.

Solve the logic puzzle to find out where each suspect bought paper and in what type of machine they used it.

Suspects	Paper King	Office Works	Wally World	Buy-A-Lot	desktop computer	electric typewriter	laptop computer	portable typewriter
Harvey Hepple								
Roscoe Ruffin								
Felix Listwell								
Loose Draw								
desktop computer								
electric typewriter								
laptop computer								
portable typewriter								

Clues

1. Roscoe always shops at Office Works.
2. The man who has an electric typewriter buys paper from Paper King.
3. Loose Draw loves his portable typewriter.
4. The man who shops at Wally World owns a laptop.
5. Felix cannot afford to buy a computer.

⇨ **How might this evidence be useful in solving the case?**

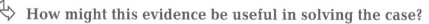

©

FINGERPRINTS

When the forensics team dusted the kennel for fingerprints they found prints on the kennel gate, door knob leading to the hall, and the door frame. Many of them matched prints for Mr. Filibuster, Harvey Hepple, and Maggie Basse, all of whom had reason to be in the kennel. They also uncovered the prints shown below. Do these match any of the suspects' prints?

Prints Found at the Kennel

| prints found on kennel gate | prints found on door knob | prints found on door frame | prints found on door frame |

Suspects' Prints

| Felix Listwell | Roscoe Ruffin | Harvey Hepple | Nicole Williamson |

☞ **Do these prints prove that one person committed the crime? Who? Why?**

Detective Notes
_____
_____

A TOOL IMPRESSION

The forensics investigators found a "jimmy" mark on the wooden jamb of the door to the kennel. A jimmy mark is an impression of a tool (a screwdriver or crowbar) that is left in the wood of a window, door, or door jamb. It is the result of a forced entry when a criminal wedges the tool between the door and its jamb while prying the door open.

A photographer from the crime lab made photographs of the jimmy mark. After processing the film, she enlarged the photograph so that the impression made by the tool would be easy to see.

After examining the photograph, Detective Barkmore reasoned that the mark was made by a crowbar. He examined the tool boxes belonging to the three remaining suspects. He found that all three men had a crowbar in their possession. He compared the tools with the photograph of the jimmy mark to find out which tool could have made the impression.

Jimmy Marks

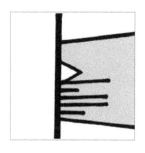

impression from the door jamb

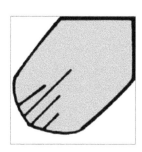

Hepple's crowbar

Ruffin's crowbar

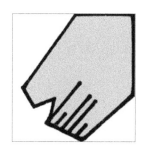

Listwell's crowbar

Detective Notes

What can you conclude from the evidence? Why?

_____

_____

The Case of the Forged Houdini
Teacher's Guide

Introduction

This is a Halloween mystery, focusing on Houdini. All facts regarding Houdini mentioned in the mystery are true. All references to other famous magicians are fictitious.

Begin the mystery by asking students what they know about Harry Houdini. List facts they know on the board. You can supplement their knowledge with facts from the *Harry Houdini Fact Sheet* (page 27). Point out the date of Houdini's death. Explain that because Houdini died on Halloween, there is to going to be a party in his honor.

Hand out the introduction that has the invitation to the costume party and information regarding the hostess, auction, and guest list (pages 28 and 29).

Prior to reading, write these two words on the board "memorabilia" and "authenticity." Discuss their meanings and explain that they will play important roles in this mystery.

The Crime

For this lesson students will need tracing paper.

Hand out "The Crime" (page 30) and "The Inscriptions" (page 31). Read the first page and discuss what students learned about the handwriting analysis. Ask students to complete the handwriting analysis activity on the second page.

Answer

They will discover that the inscription was forged.

Mixed Up Data

Ask students why specific details about time and place are important considerations when solving a crime. Discuss. Why would it be important to have these details organized in a logical order? Hand out "Talking At Once" (page 32). Ask students to read and organize the statements listed on the page in a logical sequence. When finished, ask them what these statements suggest about when the crime was committed.

Answer

1. *"Forrest Long arrived here at 6:30 p.m. to authenticate the collection for the auction," Eloise explained.*

2. *"Forrest Long told me the collection was in tip-top shape," Eloise said, "then he left just as the first guest was pulling into the drive."*

3. *"I'm always the first to arrive," Rebecca Eubanks said, "I got here tonight at 7:55."*

4. *"When I parked my car in the drive, I saw Rebecca heading up the front steps," Murdock Kane said.*

5. *"I didn't get here until 8:15," Jackson Gage stated. "I rented my costume at the last minute and ran into a crowd at the rental store."*

6. *"I was late," Johnette Street said. "I didn't get here until 8:20. I couldn't make up my mind about a costume."*

7. *"I arrived at 8:30." Wilcox Crow said. "You know, fashionably late."*

8. *"Upon arriving, we visited with one another in the living room until 8:45 when Eloise announced that it was time for dinner." Rebecca Eubanks said.*

9. *"I directed my guests to their seats at the dining room table then I told them we would view the collection in the study at 10:30, after coffee and dessert," Eloise said.*

10. *"I served the first course at 8:50," Eloise said.*

11. *"I arranged for Harris Tweet to authenticate the collection before I saw it," Murdock Kane said. "He arrived here just as the clock chimed ten o'clock."*

12. *"I had only been here about 10 minutes," Harris Tweet said, "when I discovered the forgery. I went immediately to tell Murdock."*

Ask students what these facts organized in a logical sequence suggest about when the crime was committed.

Answer

The culprit forged the inscription and stole the original book between 7:55 p.m. when the first guest arrived and 10:00 p.m. when Harris Tweet went to the study to inspect the collection.

Time of the Crime

Hand out "Time of the Crime (page 33). Ask students to read the worksheet and determine who did not commit the forgery based on this information.

Answer

Wilcox Crow is most unlikely to have committed the crime because he never left the room; therefore, he had no opportunity to forge the document or replace it with the original.

A Piece of Evidence

Ask students to read "A Piece of Evidence" (page 34) and discuss. Ask why it is important for Detective Williamson to remember the outfits Eloise and Harris Tweet are wearing.

Answer

The black fiber could possibly be from their clothing; therefore, implicating one of the guests.
It is unlikely that Murdock committed the crime since he was wearing a while linen suit.

A Stained Handkerchief

Read "A Stained Handkerchief" (page 35) and match the lip prints with the one found in the study. Why did the detective say, "If this print doesn't match the print on Eloise's napkin, I think we have a forger?"

Answer

Though Eloise didn't commit the forgery, she could have dropped a hanky with her lip print on it in her study. The two other female guests, therefore, would not be implicated in the crime and Detective Williamson would have to search for more clues.

Discuss the questions at the bottom of the page.

Answer

Rebecca Eubanks's print matched the lip print found on the handkerchief. Detective Williamson had found a black wool fiber. Rebecca was wearing a black wool cape. These things point to Rebecca being the culprit.

Resolution

Verify that students have come to the conclusion that Rebecca committed the crime.

Tell students that when she heard the evidence against her, Rebecca tried to escape from the room. She ran from the dining room and into the bathroom where she had hidden the book with Houdini's inscription in a linen closet. She grabbed the book and raced down the hall toward the kitchen, but Detective Williamson was too fast for her. He caught her and put her in handcuffs. "Too bad you're not Houdini," he said.

At police headquarters, she confessed to the crime. She stated she had wanted that book with Houdini's inscription for years. She had seen it while at Eloise's last Halloween. She had brought a copy of the book that did not have the inscription to the party. It would be easy, she reasoned, to forge this copy with Houdini's signature and switch it with the one in Eloise's study.

Since it was her first conviction, she got a light sentence. She also agreed to give her Houdini collection to the Houdini Museum in Appleton, Wisconsin, the town where Houdini was raised as a young boy.

Harry Houdini
Fact Sheet

- Houdini was born Ehrich Weiss on March 24, 1874 in Budapest, Hungary. He moved to Appleton, Wisconsin four years later with his family.

- As a boy, he loved to perform. His first act was as a trapeze artist in a neighborhood circus when he was nine. He called himself, "Ehrich, The Prince of the Air."

- His family moved to New York City in 1887.

- In 1891, Houdini and a friend formed a magic act called "The Houdini Brothers." He started calling himself "Harry Houdini."

- Harry's brother, Dash, replaced Houdini's friend in "The Houdini Brothers" act in 1893. Shortly after Dash joined him, Houdini met a performer, Beatrice Rahner. They fell madly in love and got married three weeks later. "Bess" became his partner, replacing Dash, and they changed the name of their act to "The Houdinis."

- In 1892, Houdini became known as "The Handcuff King," after developing the Handcuff Challenge Act, an act in which he challenged anyone in the audience to give him a handcuff from which he could not escape. Whoever produced the "escapeless" cuff would win $100. No one ever won the money.

- In 1900, the Houdinis went to Europe and toured there for five years.

- In 1910, Houdini was the first man to fly over Australia. After accomplishing that feat, he never flew again.

- In 1912, Houdini premiered his Chinese Water Torture Cell escape. In this he was placed head first into a tank filled with water. The lid was closed and he escaped.

- He performed "The Needle Trick." He swallowed thread and many needles then pulled them from his mouth, all the needles threaded.

- In 1926, he broke a world record when he lay submerged underwater in a sealed coffin for 90 minutes.

- Houdini became an actor and made several films during the early days of movies. In 1920, he formed his own production company, the Houdini Picture Corporation.

- Houdini used his knowledge of illusions to attempt to prove that mediums who held seances in which they claimed to contact the dead were fakes. He wrote articles about these spiritualists in which he claimed that their "contacts" were tricks.

- Houdini died on October 31, 1926 at the age of 52 from appendicitis.

- His wife, Bess, held a seance every Halloween for ten years after he died in an attempt to contact him. He told her before he died that if he could contact her after his death, he would, using a secret code. He never contacted her and she finally gave up the seances.

The Case of the Forged Houdini

The Invitation

*You are cordially invited to a
Costume Party
Halloween Night
8:00 p.m. to midnight.*

*The evening will include dinner and
a preview of the Hightower collection
of Houdini memorabilia to be sold at
auction the next day.*

✄ ✄ ✄ ✄

*At the home of Eloise Hightower
124 Hightower Road*

Come as your favorite magician.

RSVP 231-6747

The Hostess

Eloise Hightower is the widow of Harvey Hightower, a collector of Houdini memorabilia. She has a party every year on Halloween in memory of her late husband and his favorite magician, Harry Houdini. Like Houdini, her husband died on October 31. And like Houdini, Harvey died of appendicitis at age 52.

The Auction

A widow for ten years, Eloise has decided to sell her house and move to a condominium in Florida. The condo is small and Eloise will have no space to house Harvey's vast collection. She will sell the collection at an auction on November 1. All items will be examined for authenticity by Forrest Long, the world-renowned expert on Houdini. He is scheduled to examine the collection prior to the party on October 31.

The Guest List

Johnette Street   A biographer of Houdini. She has a collection of all the books that Houdini wrote. All of the books are signed by Houdini except one that will be auctioned, *The Right Way To Do Wrong, An Exposé of Successful Criminals.*

Rebecca Eubanks   Daughter of a famous magician. She has collected Houdini artifacts since she was a child. She has the largest collection of autographs by Houdini.

Jackson Gage   An amateur magician. He is proud of his collection of letters, postcards and books written by Houdini. He dreams of becoming the largest collector in the world of these items.

Wilcox Crow   A famous magician. Like Houdini, he is a master at escaping. He is called the second King of Cuffs. Houdini was the first. He has been collecting Houdini memorabilia for two years and is interested in adding to his collection, especially items that are signed by Houdini.

Murdock Kane   A master of illusion, he works at large amusement parks throughout the world and is famous for an act in which he disappears into thin air. He recently started a collection of Houdini memorabilia but worries that the items for sale are not authentic. He has arranged for his own expert, Harris Tweet, to determine the authenticity of each item at Eloise's auction.

The Crime

After all the guests arrived and greeted one another in the living room, Eloise led them into the dining room for dinner. The clock had just struck ten o'clock when Harris Tweet arrived, ready to authenticate the collection for Murdock Kane.

Eloise took Tweet to the study where the collection was located while the guests enjoyed their dessert. About ten minutes later, Tweet stormed into the dining room. Holding a book in his hand, he announced to Eloise's guests that he had spotted a forgery. He laid the book, *The Right Way to Do Wrong*, down on the table in front of Murdock, opened the book, and pointed to an inscription written on the title page. "Secure knots, Secures not — Houdini," he read aloud. He then laid a postcard from the collection beside the book. It had the same inscription.

"This is definitely Houdini's writing," he said, his index finger on the card. "But the one in the book is a forgery, and not a very good one either."

Then, Tweet drew a small notebook from his pocket, sat down in a chair, and made a chart, listing the points of handwriting analysis.

Tweet's Chart

Points of Analysis	Inscription from book	Inscription from card
proportion and size of letters		
alignment of letters		
spacing of letters and words		
letter formation (e, t, r)		
unique letters or style		

The Inscriptions

Secure Knots, secures not Houdini	*Secure Knots, secures not Houdini*
From Title Page of Book	From Postcard

Follow these steps to determine if Harris Tweet is correct.

1. To determine the proportion of the letters:
- Place a sheet of tracing paper over the inscriptions. Secure it with a paper clip.
- Make a dot at the highest point of each letter in both inscriptions.
- Remove the tracing paper and draw a line to connect the dots.
- Are the lines you drew alike or different in both inscriptions?
- Record your findings on Tweet's chart.

Secure Knots,

2. To determine the alignment of the letters and the spacing of the letters and words:
- Place another sheet of tracing paper over the inscriptions and secure.
- This time, make a dot beneath the word on the lowest parts of each letter.
- Enlarge the dot on the first and last letter of each word. Connect the dots between the letters and the words. Then, remove the paper.
- Compare the lines in both inscriptions. Are the letters written in a straight line?
- Is the spacing between the letters the same?
- Record your findings on Tweet's Chart.

Secure Knots,

3. Examine each inscription carefully.
- Are the e's looped or not looped? Are the t's crossed or not crossed?
- Are the r's pointed or arched?
- Record your findings on the chart.

e e   t t   r r

4. Are there any unique letters or letters with a dramatic style?
- Are the letters slanted to the right or left? Or are the letters straight up and down?
- Record your findings.

Based on your analysis, do you think the inscription in the book was forged?

Talking At Once

When Harris Tweet reviewed the results of his analysis with Eloise and her guests, Eloise grew pale. "A forgery," she said. "I must call the police." She turned to Harris Tweet. "Please do not let anyone leave this room."

Detective J. T. Williamson arrived at the scene in less than seven minutes. When he entered the dining room, everyone started talking to him at once.

Read each statement, then arrange them in a logical order to help Detective Williamson determine the sequence of events.

- "Upon arriving, we visited with one another in the living room until 8:45 when Eloise announced that it was time for dinner." Rebecca Eubanks said.

- "I didn't get here until 8:15," Jackson Gage stated. "I rented my costume at the last minute and ran into a crowd at the rental store."

- "I had only been here about 10 minutes," Harris Tweet said, "when I discovered the forgery. I went immediately to tell Murdock."

- "I was late," Johnette Street said. "I didn't get here until 8:20. I couldn't make up my mind about a costume."

- "Forrest Long told me the collection was in tip-top shape," Eloise said, "then he left just as the first guest was puling into the drive."

- "I arrived at 8:30," Wilcox Crow said. "You know, fashionably late."

- "I directed my guests to their seats at the dining room table then I told them we would view the collection in the study at 10:30, after coffee and dessert," Eloise said.

- "I'm always the first to arrive," Rebecca Eubanks said, "I got here tonight at 7:55."

- "I arranged for Harris Tweet to authenticate the collection before I saw it," Murdock Kane said. "He arrived here just as the clock chimed ten o'clock."

- "When I parked my car in the drive, I saw Rebecca heading up the front steps," Murdock Kane said.

- "Forrest Long arrived here at 6:30 p.m. to authenticate the collection for the auction," Eloise explained.

- "I served the first course at 8:50." Eloise said.

 After organizing and analyzing the data, when do you think the crime was committed?

Time of the Crime

After determining when the crime was committed, Detective Williamson asked Eloise if any of the guests excused themselves during the evening, leaving the living room or dining room alone.

"It seems everyone left at some point," Eloise said, "except for Wilcox. I'm certain he never did."

Detective Williamson then questioned each of the guests, recording their statements in his notebook.

Guests' Statements

Johnette Street	"I went to powder my nose right before we went to the dining room. I was gone just a few minutes."
Rebecca Eubanks	"I went to the powder room after I ate to freshen up my lipstick."
Jackson Gage	"I excused myself just after my arrival. I had to adjust my cape."
Wilcox Crow	"I didn't leave the group all night. Never needed to. I was so enjoying myself — the conversation and the food. What a night! Until this."
Murdock Kane	"I don't like sweets so I thought I'd stretch my legs after that heavy meal while the others were eating dessert. I went out on the front porch to enjoy the cool air."

 After reviewing these statements, who do you think did not commit the forgery?

A Piece of Evidence

After questioning the suspects, Detective Williamson went to the study to search for evidence that the culprit might have unknowingly left at the crime scene.

All the items in the collection were behind glass doors in tall cabinets. Detective Williamson spotted an opened door to one of the cabinets. Harris Tweet had told the detective that he had found one of the cabinet doors open when he went to the study to examine the collection. He had found the book with the forged inscription on the second shelf in that particular cabinet.

Upon inspecting the cabinet, Williamson found a tiny black wool fiber. It was caught on the metal lock on the cabinet door. "Interesting," he said, slipping the fiber into a small plastic bag. He then closed his eyes and recalled each guest, the costume that he or she was wearing, and remembered the comments some of them had made.

Party Costumes

Eloise	a bright orange dress. She said she was dressed as Bess Houdini.
Harris Tweet	beige trousers and a white shirt
Johnette Street	a short black wool witch's cape
Rebecca Eubanks	a long black wool cape like a wizard's cape – called herself Merlette, a female wizard
Jackson Gage	a long black wool cape like Gandalf might have worn
Wilcox Crow	a black wool suit
Murdock Kane	a white linen suit – said he dressed as himself

 Considering this evidence, who can be crossed off the list of possible forgers?

_____

A Stained Handkerchief

Continuing the investigation in the study, Detective Williamson spotted a white handkerchief. It was lying under a large desk. He picked it up and unfolded it. "A definite clue," he said, pointing to a red lipstick stain in its very center. "Now to find the person who blotted her lips on this hanky then unwittingly dropped it, perhaps after forging the inscription here at this desk."

Finding no other clues, Detective Williamson returned to the dining room, the handkerchief in a plastic bag in his pocket.

He picked up three paper napkins from the dining room buffet, handed them to Eloise, Rebecca and Johnette, and told them to blot their lips. He then pulled the bagged hanky from his pocket.

"If this doesn't match the print on Eloise's napkin, I think we have our forger."

He compared each lip print with the one found on the handkerchief. These were the results.

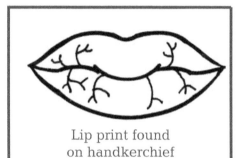

Lip print found
on handkerchief

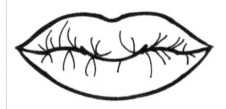

Eloise Hightower's
lip print

Johnette Street's
lip print

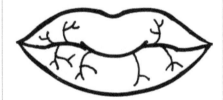

Rebecca Eubanks's
lip print

☞ **What were the results?** _____

☞ **What evidence did Detective Williamson have that pointed to the culprit?**

_____

☞ **Who was the forger?** _____

WHO TOOK THE VIDEO GAME?
Teacher's Guide

Introduction

Hand out the "Who Took the Video Game" (page 39) and have students read and discuss the crime. Call attention to Detective Caldwell's notes. Point out that notes do not have to be written in complete sentences. They are just for reference, like notes students take when doing research for a school report.

Taking Notes

Hand out "Notes About the Case" (page 40). Tell students that, like Detective Caldwell, they will need to take notes about the case. Ask students to answer the first two questions. They should keep this paper to record information as they work through the mystery.

Crime Scene

Hand out "The Crime Scene" (page 41) and discuss the evidence that was found. Discuss the fact that a crime scene should not be disturbed before it is thoroughly examined because detectives may be able to infer specific facts about the case from the evidence – source of entry, movement of the culprit within the crime scene, or clues that identify the culprit. If the evidence is disturbed, it skews these inferences and disrupts the process of determining the truth about the crime.

Explain that detectives make inferences about a case based on the factual pieces of evidence they uncover. Ask students to answer the third and fourth questions on their note sheets.

Answer

Time of crime was between 6:30 a.m. Thursday and 5:00 p.m. Friday. Because no one saw anyone around the house or in the yard, it can be inferred that the crime was most likely committed at night.
The basement window was broken and window was unlocked from inside. Based on this evidence, it can be inferred that the culprit then crawled through window.

Suspects

Hand out "Who Might Have Done It?" (page 42). After reading this page, discuss which suspects had a motive to commit the crime. Tell students to fill out the first row of the Evidence Chart on their note sheets. Discuss each suspect's motives.

Answers
- *All suspects had a motive.*
- *Van Cleff's company needs money so it can get out of the red.*
- *Rosanelle wants to start his own company so could use the holographic design.*
- *Fulbright was laid off and could sell the design for a lot of money.*
- *McDonald's company is almost out of business so he could use it to make money.*
- *Anderson could use the design as a boost to her young, fledgling company.*

Alibis

Hand out "Alibis" (page 43). Read and discuss the information on this sheet. Ask students to fill out the second row on the Evidence Chart.

Answers

Eliminate Alfredo Rosanelle as a suspect. It was substantiated that he was out of town all week.

Shoe Facts

Hand out "Shoe Facts" (page 44). Ask students to read the sheet and complete the logic puzzle.

Answer

Otis Van Cliff - 6'2" - Joggers
Gloria Fulbright - 5'9" - Runabouts
Marston McDonald - 6'0" - Air Shock
Felicia Anderson - 5'3" - Aerobic Aces
Van Cliff and Anderson can be eliminated as suspects based on both their choice of sneakers and their heights. Students may also want to eliminate McDonald. He is within the height range but did not wear Runabouts.

Then, ask students to complete the chart of notes about the case and to answer question five. Discuss all the evidence that points to Gloria Fulbright.

Answer

Fulbright had a motive. She wanted money that she could make from selling the game. She had no alibi. No one could substantiate that she was sick or where she was on Thursday and Friday. She was 5'9" and wore Runabout sneakers.

Message Decoding

Hand out "Decoding the Message" (page 45) and "A Password Disguised" (page 46). Tell students that what the detective found written on the paper are Jack's two passwords written in code. Ask students to try to decode the phone message and the grocery list.

Passwords

847-8825 spells VIRTUAL
239-2731 spells BEWARE
The grocery list spells OPEN SESAME.

The other clue for the shopping list code:
The number of items indicated on the list is the clue that tells you what letter to use. Ex. 2 ears corn - use the second letter in corn. The "o."

After Detective Caldwell decoded the messages, he called Jack and asked him if these were indeed his passwords. Jack confirmed that they were. The grocery list was the code for the password into his computer. The other was the password for the video game.

Is there enough evidence for Detective Caldwell to make an arrest? Ask students to review all of their notes before answering this question. Ask them what evidence supports their statement.

Answer

Gloria Fulbright had a motive. She wanted money that she could make from selling the game. She had no alibi. No one could substantiate that she was sick or where she was on Thursday and Friday. She was 5'9" and could have worn the sneaker that made the print. She was in possession of Jack's passwords.

Epilogue

Gloria Fulbright was arrested. Her house was searched and Jack's laptop was found in her attic. It was taken to the lab where it was analyzed. Fulbright's prints were found on it. It did not appear that Fulbright had tampered with the game design.

Gloria Fulbright broke down and confessed, saying she was so frightened because she didn't have enough money to live the lifestyle she enjoyed. She also said that Jack had angered her when he had refused to work with her on his new game. She had spent the last six months spying on him. She heard him tell his brother while they were shopping in a local grocery store that his password was written in a code. He had written them that way so they would be easy for Colin to find if something ever happened to him. He went on to say that one was a simple grocery list and the other one was two phone numbers. Both codes were kept in plain view on his desk. It was then that Gloria got the idea for the robbery.

She was sent to prison, where she taught computer programming to many of the inmates. This enabled them to get jobs when they got out of jail. Her contact with the inmates made her realize that it was more important to give to people and be of service to them than it was to take from them.

WHO TOOK THE VIDEO GAME?

Jack Basse returned home after a two-day stay in the hospital and raced down the stairs to his basement. He flipped on the light and hurried to his desk in the corner. Without bothering to sit down, he opened the right hand drawer. "I knew it!" he screamed, "I knew it! I should never have left it here. I should have taken it to the hospital with me." He slammed the drawer shut, pulled his cell phone from his pocket, and phoned the police to report the robbery.

"What was stolen?" Detective Eric Caldwell said as he stepped through the door.

"My laptop computer," Jack said. "And in it is the video game I've been working on for ten months. Someone has stolen it."

While continuing to question Jack, Detective Caldwell jotted down pertinent details about the case.

Detective Caldwell's Notes

Jack Basse
- ✓ A former employee at Virtual Videos, the top manufacturer of video games. Laid off 11 months ago. Prior to lay-off, had worked at home on a secret design for a new game – a holographic video game.

- ✓ Said it would make the whole room come alive with life-size characters. All holograms.

- ✓ An amateur cryptographer – had written the password to both his lap top and his video game in code.

- ✓ Said that once someone got into the game, they would have access to the source code (the way the game was programmed) and they could then duplicate it.

- ✓ Both passwords were in plain view on top of his desk. But both were disguised in a code – one as a shopping list, the other as two phone numbers.

NOTES ABOUT THE CASE

1. What was the crime? _____

2. Why was Jack so upset that this had happened? _____

_____

3. When did the crime take place? _____

4. How was entry made into the basement? _____

Evidence Chart

	Otis Van Cleff	Alfredo Rosanelle	Gloria Fulbright	Marston McDonald	Felicia Anderson
motive	yes				
alibi	*no*				
height					
type of sneaker					

Who committed the crime? _____

What is the evidence to support your idea? _____

_____

THE CRIME SCENE

Evidence found at the crime scene

✓ Basement window was broken and unlocked from inside.

✓ A partial footprint was found outside the basement window.

Other notes about the case

✓ Jack left for the hospital at 6:30 a.m. on Thursday. Colin, his brother, picked him up and drove him there. He lives in a town 20 miles away.

✓ Jack returned on Friday at 5:00 p.m. After putting food in his refrigerator, Colin left to go to his job at the hospital. He is a pediatrician and needed to see one of his patients.

✓ No one had a key to Jack's house except Colin.

✓ His back yard is visible to his neighbors. None of his neighbors saw anyone in his house or yard.

WHO MIGHT HAVE DONE IT?

Detective Caldwell asked Jack who might want the video game he had designed.

"I know many people who would want it," Jack said. "It's going to revolutionize this industry." He gave Detective Caldwell a list of people who he knew would want the design.

Detective Caldwell made notes as Jack told him what he knew about each person on the list.

Detective Caldwell's Notes

Suspect List

Otis Van Cleff   President of Virtual Videos. Has been in business 10 years. Didn't get some important contracts so his company is in the red. Had to lay off three of his design engineers. Jack was the first to go because he was the newest employee.

Alfredo Rosanelle   Van Cleff's partner. Has been threatening to leave Virtual Videos and start his own company. His secretary said that she had heard him say that he was frustrated working there because Van Cleff was not open to innovation.

Gloria Fulbright   Worked with Jack Basse at Virtual Videos. Was the third person to be laid off. She begged Jack to work with her on a project since they had both been laid off, but he refused. He had hinted to her about his idea while they were still at Virtual Videos but had never mentioned that it was a hologram. He hasn't spoken to her in ten months. She is currently working at a temporary job as a programmer for a large accounting firm.

Marston McDonald   President of Real Live Video Games. His company is almost out of business. Had to take a big loan to keep it afloat.

Felicia Anderson   Owner of a new video game business, six months old. Her company is making very little money. Having trouble paying her employees.

ALIBIS

Detective Caldwell asked each suspect where they were and what they were doing during the two days that Jack was in the hospital.

Otis Van Cleff   He claimed he worked until midnight Thursday night. He got to work early Friday morning and didn't leave until after 7:00 p.m.

Alfredo Rosanelle   His secretary stated that he was out of town all week. Said he was on a cruise to the Bahamas.

Gloria Fulbright   She was sick all week. She called in sick every day because she wasn't getting well.

Marston McDonald   He stated he was at work and that his wife could verify it.

Felicia Anderson   She claimed she had been very busy working for the last few days.

After questioning people to substantiate the suspects' alibis, Detective Caldwell made these notes.

Detective Caldwell's Notes

- ✓ Van Cleff's secretary stated that he was at the office both days but she did not know how late he worked each evening. His appointment book indicated that he had early appointments on Thursday and Friday mornings at 8:00 a.m. He had no appointments in the late afternoon on either of the two days.

- ✓ A woman at the Worldwide Travel Agency confirmed that Rosanelle had taken a cruise to the Bahamas.

- ✓ Gloria Fulbright's employer confirmed that Gloria had been out sick all week. Gloria lives alone and had no contact with anyone during the week to substantiate that she was actually ill.

- ✓ McDonald's wife stated that her husband got home from work at 10:45 p.m. Thursday and at 10:00 p.m. on Friday. He left for work both days around 7:00 a.m.

- ✓ Anderson's employees said they seemed to remember that she was working both days, usually arriving before 7:00 a.m. and leaving after 8:00 p.m.

 Can any suspects be eliminated because of his or her alibi? _____

SHOE FACTS

A forensic technician made a plaster imprint of the footprint found outside the basement window at the crime scene. The imprint revealed that the sneakers were made by Runabout.

He then measured the distance between the heel and the toe of the print. It was found to be between 10½ and 11 inches. The technician knew that the length of a person's foot is approximately 15 percent of his or her height. As a result, he was able to calculate the height of the person wearing the sneaker.

Technician's Calculations	15% = .15
10.5 divided by .15 = 70 inches	→ 70 inches divided by 12 = 5'8"
11 divided by .15 = 73 inches	→ 73 inches divided by 12 = 6'1"

 What was the approximate height of the person wearing the sneaker? _____

Detective Caldwell then paid a visit to the four remaining suspects to question them further. Solve the logic puzzle to determine what he uncovered during his interrogation.

	5'3"	5'8"	5'9"	6'2"	Air Shock	Joggers	Aerobic Aces	Runabouts
Otis Van Cleff								
Gloria Fulbright								
Marston McDonald								
Felicia Anderson								
Air Shock								
Joggers								
Aerobic Aces								
Runabouts								

Clues

1. Marston is taller than Gloria but is not the tallest suspect.
2. The suspect who wears Air Shocks is neither the tallest not the shortest suspect.
3. The tallest suspect wears Jogger sneakers.
4. Felicia is shorter than Gloria, who wears Runabout sneakers.

DECODING THE MESSAGE

Detective Caldwell searched Gloria's home and found two numbers written on a pad by her phone. Suspecting that they were the passwords to Jack's computer, he wrote down the two phone numbers and began to decode the message.

Use your investigative instincts to decode these coded messages.

phone numbers:	decoded message
847-8825	_____
239-2731	_____

Hint

There are 26 letters in the alphabet. The phone pad contains ten numbers. There are three letters on each number, except for number 1 and 0. Use this phone pad to help you decode the message and figure out the two passwords.

Another Hint

The most frequently used letters in the English language are
e, t, a, o, i, n, s, h, r, d, l, and *u.*
I and *a* are the only single letter words.

A PASSWORD DISGUISED

At Gloria's apartment Detective Caldwell also discovered this grocery list in a small box in her kitchen pantry. Knowing that Jack had written one of his codes as a list, he immediately began decoding this list.

Can you figure out the password by decoding the message?

coded list	item deciphered
2 ears corn	_____
2 boxes spaghetti	_____
3 loaves bread	_____
3 cans tuna fish	_____
3 packages fish sticks	_____
3 lbs. steak	_____
1 box salt	_____
4 bags potato chips	_____
3 lbs. hamburger	_____
2 heads lettuce	_____

complete message _____

Hint

Ignore all quantity labels, like ears, boxes, or loaves.

Aunt Sally's Secret
Teacher's Guide

Introduction

In this mystery, students will follow two young detectives as they uncover a hoax. Students will be presented with several pieces of evidence (many of which are printed documents) and asked to determine how these clues either verify or discredit the theory that Aunt Sally stole a ruby ring and then burned down her house to cover the crime.

Tell students that something very mysterious happened at a school in a nearby town just last week. Read the following account of what happened.

> The eighth grade students in Miss Fazzle's sixth period social studies class made an interesting discovery last Friday when they were digging on a site in the woods behind the school grounds. The dig was an activity in their study of archaeology. The site was the location of an old house owned by a woman known as Aunt Sally.

> Tales had been told about Aunt Sally for years and all of the students at the middle school had heard them. According to legend, she had died when her house burned to the ground. No one ever knew what caused the fire but police suspected arson. Legend claims that each night Aunt Sally's ghost searches the place, looking for a metal box that contains the truth about the fire.

> Several students digging near an old oak tree uncovered just such a dark green metal box. It wasn't locked so they opened it and found it contained documents and a ring with its jewel missing. Could this be the metal box Aunt Sally was searching for?

Contents

Hand out "Contents of the Metal Box" (pages 50-51). Tell students these are the contents found in the box. Ask them to examine each one very carefully. Then ask what inferences they can make from the collection. Discuss. Ask them to write down an account of what they think might have happened to the heart ruby and what role Aunt Sally played in its disappearance.

Tell students that things are not always what they seem. Hand out "Not A Thief?" (page 52). Ask the class to read and answer the questions. Discuss the evidence the two girls have found and what these things suggest.

Answer
- *Exhibit 1 - The newspaper articles couldn't have been copied on a copy machine.*
- *Exhibit 2 - The diary entries couldn't have been written with a fine point felt tip pen in 1957.*
- *Exhibit 3 - The box had to have been buried within the last week because it was purchased at Wally World, which had just opened.*

Different Documents

Hand out Exhibit 4, "A Different Set of Documents" (pages 53-54). Ask students to examine each of the documents very carefully. Lead them to compare this set of documents with the first set found in the box. Ask what discrepancies they see in the two sets of documents. What inferences can they make about Aunt Sally, her house, and the Heart Ruby? Which set of documents is real? How do they know? Discuss.

Lead the students to look at dates on both sets as clues. Another clue is the similarities in the two newspaper articles about the heart ruby dated December 20, 1956 and January 20, 1957. These similarities indicate that one of the articles was copied from the other with alterations. The photograph proves that the house was standing on June 16, 1962. Therefore, the first set is fake.

Suspects

Hand out "Who Could Have Done It" (pages 55-56). Ask students to read each set of facts. Ask them to draw conclusions based on facts presented by the girls and write their conclusions on page 56. Discuss.

Possible Conclusions
- *Fact 1 - Whoever buried the box wanted someone to find it.*
- *Fact 2 - Only the sixth period class knew that they were going to Aunt Sally's house on Friday to dig.*
- *Fact 3 - Students were eager to find something. As a result, they might be more gullible than usual.*
- *Fact 4 - If a student was guilty, he or she would had to have buried the box after school, most likely before sunset at 5:20 p.m.*

After considering the facts, students should come to the conclusion that the culprit was more than likely a member of their sixth period class and that he or she had created and buried the documents as a prank.

Which student was guilty?

Suspects

Hand out "Suspects" (page 57). Ask students to read the facts and cross out the ones that are not relevant to the case.

Answers
Facts 1, 4, 6, 7, 9, and 10 are not relevant.

Fact 2 - This fact indicates that the students live close enough to walk to Aunt Sally's after school.

Fact 3 - The student would be free to bury box after school.

Fact 5 - Students with these interests and abilities might be more inclined to pull a prank.

Fact 8 - Students probably wouldn't know that the felt-tip pen and the Xerox machine were invented after the date on the documents.

Fact 11 - Students would have access to the type of pen used to create diary entries.

Fact 12 - Students would be capable of rewriting newspaper articles and writing diary entries.

Final conclusions
Any of these students might be guilty but further evidence is needed to determine who.

More Evidence

Tell students that the detectives needed evidence to determine which of the suspects might be guilty. Hand out "More Evidence" (page 58). Ask students to read and complete the logic puzzle, combining the information supplied by the custodian and the information in the clues to complete the logic puzzle and find the person who planted the evidence.

Answer

Student	Cap	Coat	Height
Lily	black	red	5'9"
Miranda	navy blue	navy blue	5'11"
Horace	orange	green	6'0"
Otis	no hat	beige	4'1"

New Evidence

Hand out "The Truth Surfaces" (page 59). Ask students to examine the new evidence. What do these documents suggest about the case?

Answer

Miss Fazzle was behind the fake documents. She asked Horace to be her accomplice and provided him with sources to use in creating the contents for the box.

Resolution

Tell students that both Megan and Alex confronted Miss Fazzle, and she admitted that indeed she was involved in the hoax

She said, "I thought it would be a great exercise to get my students to think. Just because something is in print does not mean that it is necessarily true. You must be critical thinkers and analyze the validity of everything you read in books, newspapers, magazines and on the Internet." She then commended Alex and Megan for their fine detective work.

The Contents of the Metal Box

Washington Post   January 20, 1957

The Cursed Heart Ruby

Everyone has heard of the curse of the Hope Diamond but few know about the destruction brought to those who possess the Heart Ruby. Six carats, the ruby was cut in the shape of a heart and set in a gold ring. The Count of Bavaria had the ring made for his beloved as a valentine's gift in 1904. When he slipped the ring onto her finger, the Countess fainted from its beauty. She fell to the ground before the Count could catch her and hit her head on the marble floor. She became delirious and died the following evening.

In his grief, the Count screamed that the ruby was cursed. The ruby's history indicates the Count might have been correct. The second person who possessed the ruby died of food poisoning on her 21st birthday. The next owner of the ruby was killed when a tree crushed her body during a violent storm. The ruby then fell into the hands of a trapeze artist who died while performing a dangerous act. The last owner, Melody O'Light, said that the deaths were just coincidence and that the curse was nothing more than legend. Unfortunately, she was wrong. She died last night after choking on a chicken bone at dinner.

Who will be the next owner of this infamous jewel?

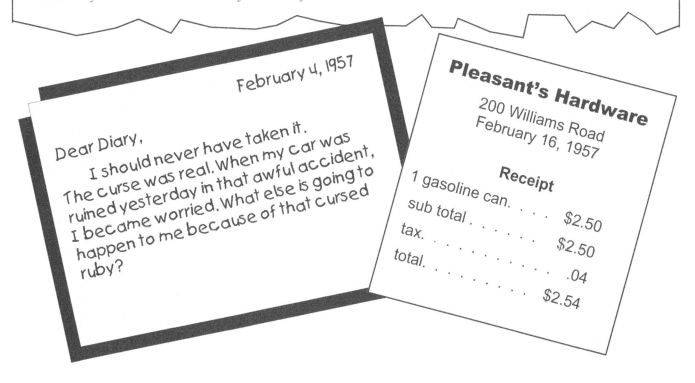

February 4, 1957

Dear Diary,
I should never have taken it. The curse was real. When my car was ruined yesterday in that awful accident, I became worried. What else is going to happen to me because of that cursed ruby?

Pleasant's Hardware
200 Williams Road
February 16, 1957

Receipt

1 gasoline can. . . . .
sub total $2.50
tax. $2.50
total. 04
                               $2.54

Washington Post   February 14, 1957

Police Narrow Search in Quest for Jewel Thief

Police announced in a press conference yesterday that they were closing in on the thief who stole the Heart Ruby. The famous jewel was stolen on February 1 from an armored truck. The ring was being transported to a safety deposit box after its owner, Melody O'Light, died in her home.

Driving a Chevrolet, the thief forced the truck off the road. A woman wearing a clown's mask and a long black skirt stepped from the vehicle with a gun in her hand. She demanded that the driver climb out and open the back door. The thief then asked for the ruby, grabbed it from a guard, and sped away. The thief's Chevrolet was found to be a rented vehicle leased from the Drive Slow Rental agency. Police are working to identify the person who rented the vehicle.

ring that was found in
the metal box

February 16, 1957

Dear Diary,
Oh no! The police have identified me as the thief. I must do something! I could never go to jail! I need to disappear somehow. I know! A fire. I'll burn my house down and everyone will think I died in the fire.

Not a Thief?

After examining the box and its contents on Friday, the students were excited.

"Aunt Sally was a jewel thief!" Horace exclaimed. "Who would have guessed?"

"I wonder where she is now?" Miranda said. "Probably she sold the ruby, which I bet was worth millions, and is living in a castle in the south of France."

On Monday the students were still talking about Aunt Sally and the crime she had committed.

"Aunt Sally wasn't a thief," Megan Williamson said, "and Alex and I have the evidence to prove it."

Miss Fazzle asked the two girls to present their evidence to the class. They presented the class with four things that they thought were suspicious.

1 "We'll call this 'Exhibit one,'" Alex Caldwell said, holding up the two newspaper articles found in the metal box. "It's obvious that these articles were photocopied, but Xerox copy machines weren't available for customers until 1959. I know this because Megan and I did a report on office inventions."

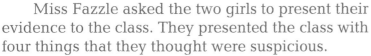 **What does exhibit one suggest about the contents in the box?** _____

2 She then held up the two diary entries. "These were written with a fine point felt-tip pen, and felt-tip pens weren't invented until 1960."

What does exhibit two suggest? _____

3 Megan held up the green box. She pointed to a price tag on the bottom. "Exhibit three," she said. "This box was bought at Wally World, which just opened last week."

What does exhibit three suggest? _____

4 Alex then handed out copies of a set of documents to the class. "Exhibit four," she said. "Ms. Wilson at the public library helped us locate these on Saturday. Look at each document carefully. "

What does exhibit four suggest? _____

Exhibit 4

A Different Set of Documents

Washington Post   December 20, 1956

THE CURSED HEART RUBY

A spokeswoman for the Smithsonian announced yesterday that the museum had acquired the Heart Ruby. Six carats, the ruby was cut in the shape of a heart and set in a gold ring. The owner of the jewel, Melody O'Light, donated the ring to the museum. The ring will be displayed in the institution's Museum of Natural History.

The value of the ring was not disclosed but collectors speculate it is worth at least five million dollars.

Like the Hope Diamond, the Heart Ruby is associated with a curse. The count of Bavaria had the ring made for his beloved as a valentine gift in 1904. When he slipped the ring onto her finger, the Countess fainted from its beauty. She fell to the ground before the Count could catch her and hit her head on the marble floor. She became delirious and died the following evening.

In his grief, the Count screamed that the ruby was cursed. The ring's history indicates the Count might have been correct. The second person who possessed the ring died of food poisoning on her 21st birthday. The next owner of the ring was killed when a tree crushed her body during a violent storm. The ring then fell into the hands of a trapeze artist who died while performing a dangerous act. Miss O'Light then purchased the ring. She reports that she has come to no harm as a result of owning the ring.

The Wilson County Gazette
May 11, 1968

HENLEY HOUSE BURNS

The old Henley farmhouse on Pearson's Corner Road burned last night. The Fire Chief said the fire was caused by outdated electrical wiring.

Doug Henley, who resided in the house, was asleep when the fire started. He called the fire department then escaped from the flames with his wife and two small children.

The house was built by Mr. Henley's family when they first moved to the county in the early 1800s.

Is this ring really cursed?

Wilson County Gazette

June 16, 1962

Oak Tree Celebrates 100th Birthday At Henley Farm

The Wilson County Gazette
September 7, 1966

Sally B. Henley died September 6. She was 70 years old. Miss Henley was a life-long resident of Wilson County and lived all of her life in her family home on Pearson's Corner Road in the county.

She is survived by two nieces, one nephew, and nine great nieces and nephews.

Who Could Have Done It?

After the students examined the new evidence, they agreed that the documents in the box were fake.

"But who would have created these fake documents and buried them and why?" Megan asked.

Being a good detective, Alex had already planned the next thing they needed to do. "In order to answer those questions," Alex said, "I think we need to consider these facts." She handed out a sheet to each student that she had typed on the computer.

1. The box was buried just below the surface of the ground. It was covered with only two or three inches of dirt. The box was buried close to the old foundation of Aunt Sally's house, a place where people would be likely to dig if looking for artifacts.

2. Miss Fazzle didn't want the students in her other classes to feel slighted because she wasn't going to take them to Aunt Sally's, so she asked her sixth period students not to tell anyone about the dig. Everyone likes Miss Fazzle, and they also like the idea that she might give them another special treat. Therefore, they would surely honor her request to keep the dig a secret.

3. Many sixth period students had expressed hope that they would dig up something that would explain how Aunt Sally had died and why her house had burned to the ground. Several had said that they hoped it was something really extraordinary.

4. The woods behind the school where Aunt Sally's house is located is off-limits to students during school hours. There are many after-school activities scheduled for Monday through Thursday afternoons from 3:00 p.m. to 5:30 p.m. Sunset last week was at 5:20 p.m.

After reading the facts that Alex presented to the class, write your ideas about what you think happened.

What conclusions can you draw from these facts?

Fact 1 _____

_____

Fact 2 _____

_____

Fact 3 _____

_____

Fact 4 _____

_____

After considering all of these facts, who do you think did it and why did he or she do it?

_____

_____

_____

_____

_____

Suspects

Miss Fazzle had assigned students to work together in groups at Aunt Sally's. Each group was free to choose where they would dig for artifacts at the site.

"In order to figure out who's guilty." Megan said. "I think we should first take a look at the students in group four. After all, they did pick the one spot on all of Aunt Sally's property to dig where the box was hidden."

"I made a list of facts about Miranda, Lily, Otis and Horace, the members of group four," Alex said. "I'm sorry to single out one group, but it seems like the most logical way to figure out who did this."

Read the following facts about the students in group four and cross out the ones that are not relevant to the case.

1. All students play some type of sport.
2. All of the students live within a quarter mile of the school.
3. None of these students have an afternoon activity on Wednesday or Thursday.
4. All of the students have been in the same school system since kindergarten.
5. One of the students is the class clown; one has always been a prankster; one loves to write mysteries; and one has a huge imagination and is always telling wild stories.
6. All students are well-liked by their classmates and teachers.
7. None of the students have pets.
8. None of those students did a report on office inventions.
9. All of the students love to read.
10. None of these students can play a musical instrument.
11. All of these students frequently use a fine point felt-tip pen.
12. All of these students are good writers.

➥ **Considering the relevant facts, can you draw any conclusions about the guilt of these students? Could they possibly be the culprits? If so, what facts support your idea?**

_____

_____

_____

More Evidence

In order to gather evidence to determine which suspect might be guilty, Alex and Megan questioned the custodian. He cleaned the classrooms in the wing of the building that faced the path to the woods. They asked if he had noticed a student near the woods either Wednesday or Thursday afternoon after school. He said he did see a person running toward the woods Thursday afternoon. He couldn't tell if it was a boy or girl, but the person was tall and was wearing a green jacket and an orange hat. He also stated that the student was carrying a shovel and a box of some sort.

Use the clues to solve the logic puzzle and solve the mystery.

	Color of Caps				Color of Jackets				Height			
	black	navy blue	orange	no hat	red	green	navy blue	beige	4'1"	5'9"	5'11"	6'0"
Lily												
Miranda												
Horace												
Otis												

Clues:

1. The shorter boy always wears a beige jacket and the shorter girl wears a red one.
2. Miranda's jacket is the same color as her cap.
3. Otis hates to wear anything on his head.
4. The two girls are taller than the shorter boy but not the taller boy.
5. Lily, the boy in the beige coat, and Horace often walk home together.
6. Miranda treated the boy in the orange hat and Lily to cookies at lunch.

The Truth Surfaces

After presenting the evidence to the class, the two young detectives confronted Horace.

"We think you created this hoax and our class deserves an explanation," Megan said.

Horace grinned. "I'm actually not the only one who's guilty," he said. He pulled out a brown envelope from his desk and spread the contents out on the table for the two detectives to examine. "After you look at these, you'll see that I mean."

Smithsonian Museum Gift Shop

Horace,
My replica of the ring looks like the real thing.

Copy Best Copies

qty	item	price	total
2	copies	.30 ea.	.60
	subtotal		.60
	tax		.03
	total		.63

Wed.

Horace,

Can you meet with me after school this afternoon? I need your help for a special class project.

Miss Fazzle

Horace,

IOU $.63 for copying at Copy Best.

Miss Fazzle

Washington Post
December 20, 1956

Horace — This is the article I told you about that would work for us. It just needs a few changes.
Miss Fazzle

THE CURSED HEART RUBY

A spokeswoman for the Smithsonian announced yesterday that the museum had acquired the Heart Ruby. Six carats, the ruby was cut in the shape of a heart and set in a gold ring. The owner of the jewel, Melody O'Light, donated the ring to the museum. The ring will be displayed in the institution's Museum of Natural History.

The value of the ring was not disclosed but collectors speculate it is worth at least five million dollars.

Like the Hope Diamond, the Heart Ruby is associated with a curse. The Count of Bavaria had the ring made for his beloved as a valentine gift in 1904. When he slipped the ring onto her finger, the Countess fainted from its beauty. She fell to the ground before the Count could catch her and hit her head on the marble floor. She became delirious and died the following evening.

In his grief, the Count screamed that the ruby was cursed. The ring's history indicates the Count might have been correct. The second person who possessed the ring died of food poisoning on her 21st birthday. The next owner of the ring was killed when a tree crushed her body during a violent storm. The ring then fell into the hands of a trapeze artist who died while performing a dangerous act. Miss O'Light, then purchased the ring. She reports that she has come to no harm as a result of owning the ring.

Writing Matrix Logic Puzzles

Follow these easy steps to write logic puzzles. Then, get a friend to solve them.

1. Decide on four characters in your puzzle. Write their names in the first column.
2. Decide on an attribute pertaining to your characters like height, hair color, likes, dislikes. Write this information in the top row. For example, if you chose hair color, write brown, black, red, blonde in the boxes in the top row.
3. Decide which attribute matches each character. In other words, make up the answers to the puzzle. Write them down.
4. Now, you are ready to write the clues to your puzzle. Don't make the puzzle too difficult but also don't make it too easy.

names ↓ *attributes* →				

Clues

_____

_____

_____

_____

_____

_____

_____

Writing More Difficult Puzzles

Follow the same steps in writing a more difficult puzzle. This time, decide on two attributes for each character and add one or two more characters. Use the two-prong matrix for this puzzle.

Clues

_____

_____

_____

_____

_____

_____

_____

_____

Classification of Fingerprints

Currently, the F.B.I. has over 250 million sets of prints. Some of these are known criminals whose prints have been taken when they were arrested. Other prints are government workers or those who have applied for government jobs.

The skin on our fingers, palms of our hands, and the soles of our feet are covered with tiny lines called ridges. These ridges provide friction which helps us in picking up objects and holding onto things. These ridges form patterns. Like snowflakes, the pattern these ridges form is unique for each individual.

Fingerprints are classified according to the patterns the ridges form on our fingers. There are three major types of patterns.

Arch
The ridge lines start on one side of the finger and form an arch as they make their way to the other side.

Loop
Ridge lines start on one side and loop back to the same side.

Plain Whorl
The ridge lines form circles. They do not begin and end on either side of the finger.

Plain Arch
The ridges form a rounded arch.

Radial Loop
The ridge lines start from the right side and loop back to the right.

Central Pocket Loop Whorl

Tented Arch
The ridges form a pointed arch.

Ulnar Loop
These lines start from the left and loop back to the left.

Double Loop Whorl

Accidental Whorl

Make a Set of Fingerprints

Materials Needed

- no. 2 lead pencil
- white paper
- clear tape

Procedure

1. Use the number 2 lead pencil and color an area about the size of the end of your thumb on a sheet of paper. Color the area very dark.

2. Lay the upper part of your right thumb (from the knuckle to the tip) down on the colored area. Slowly roll your thumb from left to right. The lead from the paper will rub off onto your thumb.

3. Stick a piece of clear tape onto your thumb. Then, pull off the tape and lay it on another sheet of paper. Do you see your print?

4. Label the print "right thumb."

5. Repeat the process for all of your fingers, making sure to label each one.

5. Then, using the Fingerprint Classification Sheet, classify each of your prints. Are all of your fingers the same pattern?

Graph the Prints

1. Compare your right thumb print with that of your classmates. Make a graph to illustrate the number of whorls, loops and arches in your class.

2. How many of your classmates have the same type of pattern on both thumbs? Make a graph to illustrate this data.

Research Fingerprints

1. Research to find out who was the person who first classified prints for use in solving crimes and in identifying people.

2. Research to find out how the ancient Chinese used fingerprints.

Foot Measurements

When you become a fully-grown adult, the length of your foot will be approximately 15 percent of your height. Is that true now? Do the following activity with a partner to find out.

Directions

1. Take off your shoe and ask your partner to measure the length of your foot from your heel to the tip of your longest toe. Write it down in inches.

2. Stand against the wall. Ask your partner to measure your height in inches.

3. Now, do the following calculations:
   Divide the length of your foot by your height.
   Multiply your answer by 100.
   What did you get?

4. Complete steps one through three, this time measuring your partner.

5. Compare your results with other teams. If you and your classmates were adults and did the same calculations, each one of you would get 15 after you multiplied your answer by 100. Remember, this is because the length of an adult's foot is approximately 15 percent of his or her height. Ask your teacher to prove this by measuring his or her foot and height.

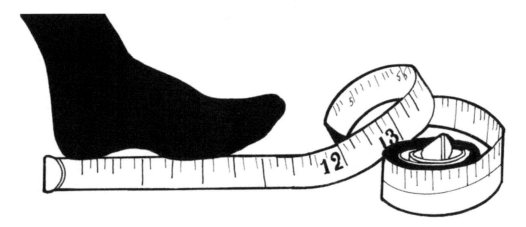

Another Thing To Do

1. Extend your arms out to the side. Ask your partner to measure the length from the tip of your middle finger on the left hand to the tip of the middle finger on your right. How does this measurement compare to your height?

2. Do the same for your partner? What are your findings?

3. Compare your findings and the findings of other teams.

4. When you are grown, the length of your arm span (the distance from fingertip to fingertip) will approximate your height. Again, ask your teacher to prove this by measuring his or her arm span and height. For further collaboration, ask your parents to do the same at home.

More One-Hour Mysteries

All lessons in this book align to the following standards.

Grade Level	Common Core State Standards in ELA-Literacy
Grade 4	RF.4.3 Know and apply grade-level phonics and word analysis skills in decoding words RF.4.4 Read with sufficient accuracy and fluency to support comprehension.
Grade 5	RF.5.3 Know and apply grade-level phonics and word analysis skills in decoding words. RF.5.4 Read with sufficient accuracy and fluency to support comprehension.

www.ingramcontent.com/pod-product-compliance
Ingram Content Group UK Ltd.
Pitfield, Milton Keynes, MK11 3LW, UK
UKHW012331270225
455677UK00027B/811